Life at Home

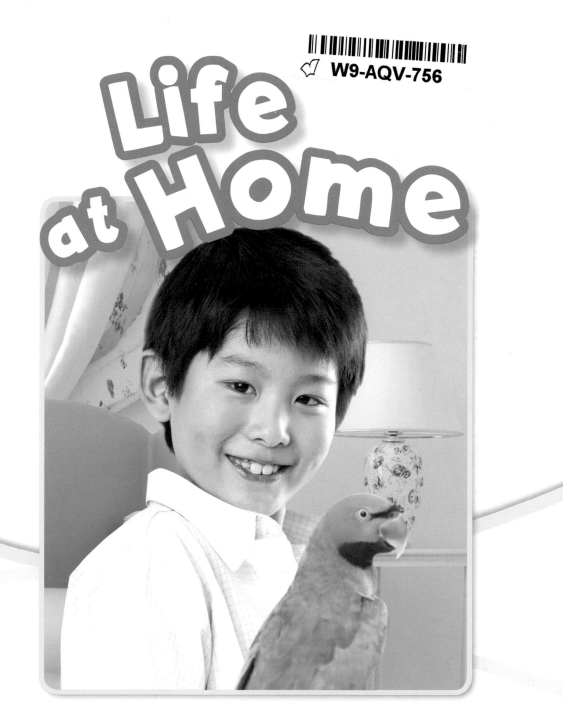

Sharon Coan, M.S.Ed.

They live in a big **city**.

We live in a big city.

This is their home.

This is our home.

They cook dinner.

We cook dinner.

They wash dishes.

We wash dishes.

They buy clothes.

We buy clothes.

They go many **places**.

We go many places.

They play with
friends.

We play with
friends.

They like their home.

We like our home.

Draw It!

1. Think about your home.

2. What do you do at home?

I play in the yard.

3. Draw a picture.

Glossary

city—a large town

places—parts of the world

Index

Your Turn!

Home is a special place. What do you like about your home? Tell a friend.

Consultants

Shelley Scudder
Gifted Teacher
Broward County Schools

Caryn Williams, M.S.Ed.
Madison County Schools
Huntsville, AL

Publishing Credits

Conni Medina, M.A.Ed., *Managing Editor*

Lee Aucoin, *Creative Director*

Torrey Maloof, *Editor*

Lexa Hoang, *Designer*

Stephanie Reid, *Photo Editor*

Rachelle Cracchiolo, M.S.Ed., *Publisher*

Teacher Created Materials

5301 Oceanus Drive
Huntington Beach, CA 92649-1030
http://www.tcmpub.com
ISBN 978-1-4333-7338-1